Venezuela

by Ariel Factor Birdoff

Consultant: Marjorie Faulstich Orellana, PhD
Professor of Urban Schooling
University of California, Los Angeles

BEARPORT
PUBLISHING

New York, New York

Credits

Cover, © ASIFE/iStock and © jimmyvallalta/iStock; TOC, © Natalia Kuzmina/Shutterstock; 4, © Vadim Petrakov/Shutterstock; 5T, © DanielAzocar/iStock; 5B, © tane-mahuta/iStock; 7, © DanielAzocar/iStock; 8T, © Fabian Michelangeli/AGE Fotostock; 8B, © Xinhua/Alamy; 9, © MaRabelo/iStock; 10L, © De Agostini Picture Library/Bridgeman Images; 10–11, © Rjcastillo/CC BY-SA 4.0; 11R, © Dani Carlo/Prisma/AGE Fotostock; 12, © FSTOPLIGHT/iStock; 13T, © John Platt/Dreamstime; 13B, © SeppFriedhuber/iStock; 14, © John Vanderlyn/Architect of the Capitol; 15T, © Jorge Silva/Reuters/Newscom; 15B, © casadaphoto/Shutterstock; 16–17, © Eagleflying/Dreamstime; 18, © Kristina Mahlau/Dreamstime; 19, © Jaromir Chalabala/Shutterstock; 20, © apomares/iStock; 21T, © Julie Feinstein/Dreamstime; 21B, © unpict/Shutterstock; 22, © Jose J. Lugo A./CC BY-SA 4.0; 23, © Daniel Romero/VWPics/Alamy; 24, © Jorge Silva/Reuters/Newscom; 25, © Pacific Press/Alamy; 26L, © Xinhua/Alamy; 26–27, © Cesar De Moya/El Nacional de Venezuela/Newscom; 28T, © Anette Linnea Rasmussen/Dreamstime; 28B, © OJO Images Ltd/Alamy; 29, © katjen/Shutterstock; 30T, © Rustik76/Dreamstime and © Andreylobachev/Dreamstime; 30B, © Vadim Petrakov/Shutterstock; 31 (T to B), © Eagleflying/Dreamstime, © Cesar De Moya/El Nacional de Venezuela/Newscom, © Carlos Alavrez/Dreamstime, and © railway fx/Shutterstock; 32, © spatuletail/Shutterstock.

Publisher: Kenn Goin
Senior Editor: Joyce Tavolacci
Creative Director: Spencer Brinker
Design: Debrah Kaiser
Photo Researcher: Thomas Persano

Library of Congress Cataloging-in-Publication Data

Names: Birdoff, Ariel Factor, author.
Title: Venezuela / by Ariel Factor Birdoff.
Description: New York, New York : Bearport Publishing, 2019. | Series: Countries we come from | Includes bibliographical references and index.
Identifiers: LCCN 2018009278 (print) | LCCN 2018009561 (ebook) | ISBN 9781684027347 (ebook) | ISBN 9781684026883 (library)
Subjects: LCSH: Venezuela—Juvenile literature.
Classification: LCC F2308.5 (ebook) | LCC F2308.5 .B57 2019 (print) | DDC 987—dc23
LC record available at https://lccn.loc.gov/2018009278

For more information, write to Bearport Publishing Company, Inc., 45 West 21st Street, Suite 3B, New York, New York 10010. Printed in the United States of America.

10 9 8 7 6 5 4 3 2 1

Contents

This Is Venezuela

Breathtaking

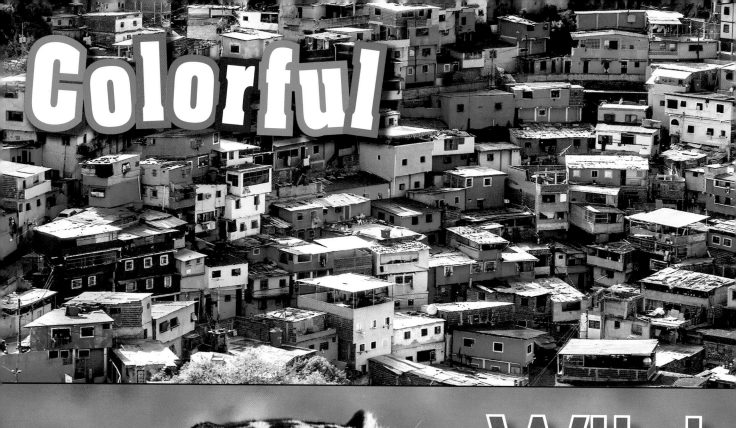

Colorful

Wild

5

Venezuela is a large South American country.

It's twice as big as the state of California!

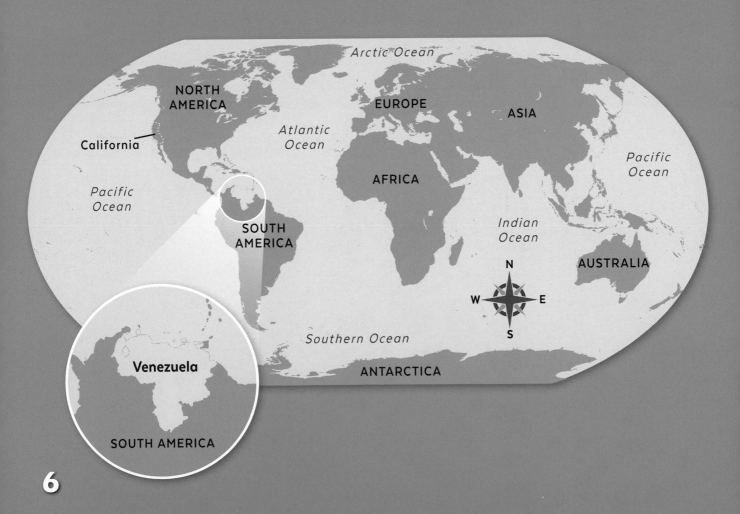

Arctic Ocean

NORTH AMERICA

EUROPE

ASIA

California

Atlantic Ocean

Pacific Ocean

Pacific Ocean

AFRICA

SOUTH AMERICA

Indian Ocean

N

AUSTRALIA

W   E

S

Southern Ocean

ANTARCTICA

Venezuela

SOUTH AMERICA

Nearly 32 million people live in Venezuela.

Venezuela's land is stunning. The country has thick forests and huge mountains.

The Catatumbo River is famous for lightning. There are over 250 lightning strikes there yearly!

lightning in Catatumbo

Some mountains have flat tops.

They are known as *tepuis* (tay-PWEE).

For thousands of years, people have lived in Venezuela.

Early settlers included the Carib and the Timoto-Cuica people.

This clay figure from Venezuela is more than 1,000 years old!

The Timoto-Cuicas built villages in valleys. They farmed the land.

The Carib people still live in parts of Venezuela. They speak a language called Carib.

11

Venezuela is bursting with life!
The country is home to many
plants and animals.

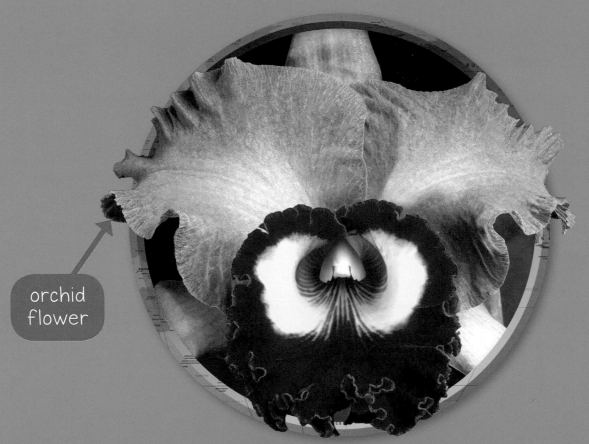

orchid
flower

The **national** flower is the orchid (OHR-kid).

Venezuela's most famous bird is the troupial (TROO-pee-uhl).

troupial

The largest rodent in the world lives in Venezuela. It's called a capybara.

capybaras

13

In 1498, Christopher Columbus saw Venezuela from the ocean.

Soon after, the Spanish took control of the land.

In 1811, Venezuela won its **independence** from Spain.

Independence Day is celebrated on July 5.

Venezuela's Independence Day

a statue of Simón Bolívar

A man named Simón Bolívar (1783–1830) helped drive the Spanish out of Venezuela.

15

Caracas is Venezuela's largest city.
It's also the country's **capital**.

Caracas

Other large cities are Maracaibo, Valencia, and Maracay.

Over 40 languages are spoken in Venezuela.

The main language is Spanish.

This is how you say *mountain* in Spanish:

Montaña (mohn-TAN-yah)

This is how you say *sun* in Spanish:

Sol (SOLE)

The Carib word for sun is *weju* (WEH–yuh).

Venezuelan food is tasty.

A popular meal is *hallaca* (ah-YAH-cah).

It's made with meat and vegetables.

You serve it on a banana leaf!

hallaca

Arepas (ah-RAY-pahs) are grilled corn cakes.

They are stuffed with meat, eggs, or cheese.

Yum!

arepas

One shop in Venezuela has 900 kinds of ice cream. It even has a flavor called hot dog!

Venezuelan musicians play *joropo* (huh-ROH-poh).

It's a kind of folk music.

The *joropo* was introduced by Spanish settlers.

Dancers twirl around.

They stomp their feet to the music.

What's the most popular sport in Venezuela?

Baseball!

In Spanish, baseball is called *béisbol*. It's pronounced the same way as in English.

Venezuelans also enjoy soccer. Fans cheer for their country's team.

Lots of **festivals** are celebrated in Venezuela.

The most colorful is *Carnaval.*

People dress up and dance in the streets!

In July, Venezuelans celebrate *Día del Niño.* It's a holiday that honors children!

Christmas is a big holiday in Venezuela.

How do people celebrate?

Many roller-skate to church!

In Spanish, Christmas is called *Navidad* (nah-vee-DAHD).

Others set off dazzling fireworks!

Fast Facts

Capital city: Caracas

Population of Venezuela:
Almost 32 million

Main language: Spanish

Money: Venezuelan bolívar

Major religion:
Roman Catholic

Neighboring countries:
Brazil, Guyana, and Colombia

Cool Fact: The highest waterfall in the world is Venezuela's Angel Falls. It's more than twice as tall as the Empire State Building!

capital (KAP-uh-tuhl) a city where a country's government is based

festivals (FES-tuh-vuhls) celebrations

independence (in-duh-PENN-duhnss) freedom

national (NASH-uh-nuhl) having to do with the whole country

Index

Read More

Schuetz, Kari. *Venezuela (Blastoff! Readers: Exploring Countries).* New York: Scholastic (2012).

Willis, Terri. *Venezuela (Enchantment of the World).* New York: Scholastic (2013).

Learn More Online

To learn more about Venezuela, visit
www.bearportpublishing.com/CountriesWeComeFrom

About the Author

Ariel Factor Birdoff is an outreach librarian in New York City. She lives in Queens with her husband and a lot of books. She loves to travel and hopes to visit as many countries as possible.